This Natal House

Small Harbor Publishing

Cover art: Mandy Rogers Horton, "Then Again for the First Time"
Interior design: Brianna Chapman
Editor: Jessie Truong
Publisher: Allison Blevins
Director: Kristiane Weeks-Rogers

THIS NATAL HOUSE
J.L. CONRAD
ISBN 978-1-957248-49-3
Harbor Editions,
an imprint of Small Harbor Publishing

This Natal House

J.L. Conrad

Harbor Editions
Small Harbor Publishing

for Elliot and Noah, always

Contents

This Natal House

In this plot I am bound to others
before being tied to my body
—Emmanuel Levinas

the subject itself: the wild velocity of motherhood,
an enforced momentum forbidding contemplation
—Sarah Manguso, *Ongoingness*

Postlude

or, last things first

He is born in the year
the world is supposed to end.

I avoid horoscopes because
I do not want to know how it will all
turn out.

Pain centers itself in the spine.
Toes wind and unwind. The back arches.

There is a tendency to remove oneself
from the site of trauma, to speak
of oneself as another.

A wet cloth on the forehead.
On the television—is this possible?—a crackling fire.

When we leave the room, there are
towels on the floor, water in the tub, white sheets
tangled on the bed.

But that isn't right. The bed leaves too.
I am on the bed.

Then, laid out on a table, arms strapped.

White lights glaring
overhead. See the blue curtain.
What happens on the other side

remains invisible to my eyes but clear
to everyone else.

I'm afraid that I won't wake up I say.
Frankly, it was hard to leave you there you tell me later.

Hear the cry. The doctor's hands
working on him in the corner.

He comes out willing. Ravenous,
as if the pressing of birth had pressed into him
a deep hunger. He does not seem angry.

Later, his profile in the bassinet,
a slant of light on the brick wall beyond
the window. *Is this the eclipse?*
I remember asking.

I cannot tell you if I fed the baby.
The records say that I did feed the baby.

There are visitors.
There are photographs of these visitors.
The visitors are known to me.
The grandmother wears a light yellow shirt.

Children born on eclipses are intense, caught between
two worlds, one foot in each.

I measured my life
by that date, thinking
by then I will be ready only
I was not.

A watery half-moon, its light in reeded strips.

*

Once upon a time there was a baby and the baby was a fish. The baby was a fish and it was swimming. At first the fish was so tiny the swimming could not be felt. As the fish got bigger, it bumped into the walls of its chamber. The bumps felt like whispers and, later, began to resemble the feeling one gets when an eyebrow twitches of its own accord. Finally, the fish grew up against the walls that contained it. The fish was a goldfish in a bag that a girl won by throwing a ring over a bottle at the county fair. The fish slipped and shimmered; it spun without stopping. The girl did not leave the fish on top of the car in the hot sun. Instead she carried it with her, the plastic loop of the bag gripped tightly in her palm. The fish had lungs but found he could breathe underwater. Fluid moved through the cavities of his body. Once upon a time there was a fish and the fish became a baby.

Blood Orange

I opened the door but you did not enter.

It is easiest to blame the angel.
Fact: a woman who walks beneath its outstretched wings
will miscarry.

There is no leavetaking
but that which the body allows.

You will experience bleeding
and some relief.
You will feel something as it passes.

The moonflower transposes its face onto darkness.

The tendency to see everything as a sign
is a sign.

The time for sending thank you notes has passed.

Your body is capable
only of letting go.

Poem in Which a Decision Has Been Reached

One Tuesday furled on another. It is
a Jubilee year, complete with waterskis and a cake
ten layers high. Our niece is a carousel horse
named Jewel Diamond Flowers. She has gold hooves
and wants to head toward the playground
where a hunger moon approaches, grimacing.
We find ourselves in heavy foot traffic. Time slows
to a muddle. *The houseplants* you are saying
when I turn them around, I feel like a god. All those faces.
It has come down to this: the bright seed
taking root in the body's damp heat.
This thick-skulled darkness heading into night.

Dearest Sweet Potato,

*Week 18: your baby is now about the size of a sweet potato—
and his tiny fingers now have unique fingerprints!*
— from "How Big is Your Baby This Week?"

How to write of your firm skin,
the milky liquid you exude on peeling?

The filaments of your flesh
have stitched themselves together.

You are the opposite of transparent.
You do not give way under fingertips.

Where were you wrested from the soil,
that moist cavity that held you close,

then closer? How far did you travel
to be here, now, in this moment?

I do not wish violence upon you,
I wish only to know you: each hint

and crevice. Do not keep secrets, I say,
though you cannot help this, having

no words with which to reveal
your inner life. What is it

that you dream, when you dream?
Do you wish again for confinement?

There is a heft to your frame, a
solidity that, even now, seems

on the increase. You were there.
You are here. That is the mystery.

Expecting

I had been expecting
so it was not a surprise when
                        the smell of hazelnuts
            lemon balm and lavender

The song brought back his dying
as if we could claim it

the move was a false one
            inhibit/inhabit
            separate the papers

I could not find any licorice
                        until the dust
            until asters

the road turning and turning through the woods
                        not wanting anything but
            the scent of
                        the sound of

When they asked did the baby move
            I was expecting

            So much for the
We will make for you a

What It Is Like

Branch curled like a wishbone
on the sidewalk.

Bones clicking each time
the heel of my right foot

strikes the pavement.
The perfect curve of the baby's skull.

If by *skull* you mean
the bone that pressed against my bones,

and if by *scalp* you mean
that which was punctured and bruised

but healed later, and if by *mouth*
you mean that which emerged ready and willing,

then this would describe the beginning.
Bricks luminous at the moment of eclipse.

I don't usually do this part the nurse says.
A feeling like sand at the back of the neck.

The spine an hourglass.
The bruise on the baby's head

an unwelcome guest. Likewise
the scar. Afternoon light leaks

from a windowframe.
You should write this down

someone tells the husband
because she won't remember.

She will ask the same questions again.
The tight fists of peonies unfurl.

Eight Years Back

There is a certain order
in which things must be done.

The rawest truth is
I should not still be alive.

The body submerged.
The two hearts beating.

Also, the body in agony.
The body struggling to expel

the baby. Tired, so that
the breath, that friend, seems

ready to depart. All eyes
on the theater. She wants

to disappear. There are helpers,
but no one moves. All night

the light drains from surfaces.
The body dehiscing

in the half-light. Machines
say the baby is fine

and then not-fine. Things,
after that, move swiftly.

The body headlong.
The body present at the scene.

The body without release.
Later there is proof

of things gone wrong
but also right. The body lashed

and stapled. The stillness
after storm. We sleep

for nearly a day. I have missed
everything I would wish

later to recall. And this
is just the beginning.

* *

Once upon a time there was a baby who became lost in the woods. Every way he turned, he saw the thick trunks of trees, dark patches of shadow, and no way out. The path untangled itself into a small clearing which seemed to be an end of sorts. The baby did not cry. Instead, he stared silently at the branches above coursing in an invisible wind that did not reach the forest floor. He lay on a bed of roots that were not soft like moss. They seemed to be telling him *Go, little one.* The baby did his best to leave this small clearing but found he could not. Every way out tangled with underbrush. The way in overgrown. So he waited.

Anterograde

Tell me again how it goes.
At the day's opening, a baby.

A slippage, as if underwater, and
the fear of not waking.

We waited for the best time.
I was never the only one in the room.

Now, the baby sleeps in front of
a tree strung with lights. The dog

settled beneath a line of paper snowflakes.
How strange I remark *to have lived*

a whole day and not remember
despite all the evidence.

Lately, I have taken to making
one cup of tea, then another.

A dream of three women on an escalator.
That was before you had your children one said.

Skin knits itself across, nerves re-
joining. The scent of cedar-or-is-it-spruce.

Recognize that some things are not lost
to you. The baby's skin *sweet like honey*

the child is saying. We are removing
all traces of _____ from the busy house.

It's a little late to be asking such questions
you tell me. I say *have you ever felt*

anything so soft? It is true there was
always going to be an egress window.

After the Rain

Combed-cotton sky.
I stop the car

to move the turtle
the rest of the way

across pavement. Baby
and dog strapped

in the backseat,
someone coming

from the opposite
direction. Hills blush

with blue-green. Birds
the first thing and last.

Each moment's soft
underbelly exposed.

Packing the Suitcase

You are a good mother. You balance the new baby along your left arm, his head resting in your cupped palm, his small limbs relaxed. You are packing the suitcase. It is time to go home from the hospital. Look how capable you are, packing the suitcase and holding the baby. There is a car seat on the bed. Soon, the new baby will be tucked in place, shielded from any harm. The husband has gone down the hallway; you are alone with the baby in the room. Soon they will come by to make sure the baby is strapped in the right way. You think to yourself *I can do this*. The baby a strange, heavy weight on your arm. As you lean over the bed to put something in the suitcase, the baby's weight tips to the side. He tips and you cannot catch him. It is both slow and fast. He falls into the car seat, lands on his side. There is a blank where your mind should be. You have just dropped the baby. No one is in the room except for you and the baby who you have just dropped. You are a bad mother. You pick up the baby and move down the bright hallway looking for your husband and the nurse who will know what to do. The baby is not even crying.

Afternoons Thick as Shuttle Cakes

For I know the difference
between *was* and *is.*

Tomorrow's thoughts out the window.
You have never spent so much time in one place.

The mute clockwork of his fingers. His steady pulse.
The way, on waking, he seems to swim

his limbs into motion, plying the air as if
tearing it apart.

Nights separated by the long thick wing of the pillow.
Sheets wicking away the body's heat and shiver.

Everything fading when
painkillers travel the chutes of the body.

The ridges on your thumbnails grow slowly out.
When the body experiences a great shock.

You do not know if you could do it all again.
The difference was

asking of your body
more than it could give.

Premonition

In this season of edging
toward spring, bowed clouds gather
near the sun's pastille. In two days, a baby

will emerge kicking. Meanwhile, snow
stretches from that horizon to this one—

interrupted by the fenceline and
a few tall weeds. Children scoop a hideout
into the snow pile's flank, which

collapses with the plow's approach.
Hours later, a passerby sees arms

flung up like flags through the crust, finds
the two boys underneath cold but unharmed.
I remove snow from the baby evergreen

with my bare hands, then use a glove
to brush the branches gently.

I have remorse for certain chapters
of my life but not this one: the time spent
near the lake with its scrim of fog,

hills stretched tawny behind. How I lived
full in my body that I did not know

would fail me, the body
seamed and sutured, the body with

its winter trees. Settled in for the long haul,
I lie here waiting, evening light
pooling in the room's corner that is

a gradual curve of plaster. I am broken down
but not dismayed. My fears have shrunk to pinpoints

like constellations. We press our feet into
snow outside the door, hold on for
the growth swelling beneath it, unseen.

Ghost of a Ghost

The bowl of the prairie.
Snowstarscatter.

All you needed was
to be embodied.

We had lived too long
alone, nothing weighting us.

Today, birds—
thick black crows

threading the air
with their dots and dashes.

The mouth opens
and closes. I keep losing

my thoughts but also
objects and intent.

All you needed was
a body to call your own.

I could not keep you together.
A cone of light funneling.

*   *   *

Once upon a time the baby who was not yet a baby dreamed. Because he had not seen the world, he dreamed shades of light and shadow. He dreamed sounds and motion: the shift of his mother's weight from foot to foot as she walked, the change from horizontal to vertical that he could sense at times. He dreamed of the life before this one. How once he had moved effortlessly among something like *flowers*, had felt wind lift and fall. As he dreamed, he felt a vague desire to become *more*. He lifted above the rounded belly of his mother, holding himself over her body in the dim light. A thin silver cord connected them. He knew somehow that he could not let it go and so sank back into the darkness that lately had surrounded him. The steady thrum of her heartbeat was, if he could have explained this, a comfort.

Poem of Creaturely Plenitude

There is pain and the remission of pain. At the zoo
the second giraffe has died. *Euthanasia* the newscaster says

and *degenerative joint condition*. In our home there is
a child where once the thought of a child

existed and is now reality. Rain moves all blue
and green across the weather-map and we have

wind-up flashlights to take to the basement. We just need
a Saturday to clean and some extra food for the pets

to keep in storage and surely we'll survive what's coming.
We do not talk about the flecks of dust that rest

in each other's eyes or that month three years ago
in which our cat stretched out her dying. Our chickens

are entering their second winter and our son
behind his wooden slats cries

because he cannot turn over. As for me, I latch onto
this new dream with both of us in it. There is

the way you look at me from your chair
and also the giraffe's head pressing its cheek

to the ground and the fur—yes, fur!
on its ossicones. There is no way to know

who knocks at the door before the knocking
is done. To write the ending before it arrives.

The C-Section

You are given socks
before entering the room—

gray with white
crosses on the soles.

The light is gray, the opposite
of morning. It could be

any time at all but in fact
is morning and you

are there for the event.
They have prepared

your body, measured
your heart and the baby's.

The room cluttered
with apparatuses.

For instance, machines
to give notice if

your blood pressure falls
too low. Sharp instruments

on a metal tray. Stainless
cabinets holding

items for every eventuality.
Also a needle for your spine.

Sit on the table they say.
Round your back.

Something has been done
to your body.

You should feel pressure
but not sharp or cold they tell you.

A man is holding
a glove filled with ice

to the bottom of your ribs
saying *Can you feel this?* and *This?*

And you are saying *yes* and *yes.*
Now there is a small mask

for your face, and air
that tastes faintly metallic.

The best thing you can do
right now he says *is breathe.*

This is the place where time
funnels to a still point.

The present viewed
as if telescopically,

the wrong end at the eye.
Are you ready they are asking.

Postpartum

What's done is done. The cat slinking
along the back fence, mouth

feathered. My body failing by degrees.
Don't worry about tomorrow.

Each day has enough. Trouble, that is.
I name this *the day of no regrets*.

How is it that each sparrow still looks
to the feeder, months empty?

Animals know what's coming to them.
Or don't. Running heedless

across streets. Two bodies I found.
One, the gray cat curled next to the signpost.

Two, the squirrel splayed belly up.
A mother, clearly. Let us live like this matters.

Arteries narrowing to a whim.
Blood thrumming through its acres.

This Place

I can see your skeleton face
beneath your skin.

It's those words I want
to take back. Slip them sideways
          under the door.

The key: as if overturned.

Within the room's heave
and shimmy: darkness.

The room a whirlpool, a star
with no center. People come and go,

but you stay. The sky
beyond the glass doors
          like a bruise.

Looking back I can see
there is no reason to be ashamed.

Mornings Like This One

You wake to the child
asking you to   *get out of bed*
and the body   to which you are tied.

You have never liked the word
        disabled.   You are lucky
you tell yourself   to have

        this husband who
will get out of bed   administer
    breakfast to the child   get
        the baby   so that you

can take the first   steps across the room
        that   in between mornings
you tell yourself   are   *not that hard.*

Fortunately the child   does not notice
        and the husband   is willing.

    This is   *not your fault*   this is
        maternity,   suffering for another
though you would never say
    to the child or the baby   *you did this.*

Place your feet   inches ahead
    lower yourself   to the blue chair
tell yourself   *in just a few minutes.*

The body, as always, resists.

There is the child careening   from
    one end of the house   to the other.

The baby in the husband's arms
opening his eyes   as he is transported
    from his bed   *as if by magic*   to

a space in the air near your body.
    His gaze   locks on yours
        as if seeing for the first time—

a smile suffuses his face that says   *you!*

for Noah, whose name means *rest* or *respite*

You are heavy with water, which means
you are still alive. How soon, on dying,
the body begins to release its weight

as one does in sleep with each exhalation,
atoms marrying themselves to atoms, carbon to
oxygen, why we wake lighter each morning.

I no longer check to see if you are breathing
when I enter your room, having shifted instead
into this new accounting of things—

whether the animals stand lined up
precisely where I left them while easing
you into sleep. Expiration, they call it,

when the spirit takes its leave. The heart,
stirring the blood's specific gravity, flinging
it through the body's farthest reaches before

calling it back home again. You, my child,
lying like an open parenthesis near the door
where I must step over you to enter. Most mornings

you wake angry, your voice recalling to me the arch
of your back in your crib and what seemed pure
indignation at being forced to wear a body.

Yet here we are, me and you, you and me,
these years later, chests rising and falling. Our hearts,
those dumb pieces of meat, still thudding along.

* * * *

Once upon a time there was a bird who stopped to visit the baby. It perched on the edge of the bassinet, spreading its wings to catch the sun. The baby's forehead in shadow. One day the bird wears its leg bound to its chest. It stands awkwardly, slipping from side to side on a single clawed foot as the baby's eyes follow its movements. Blood has begun to seep through the thin strips of white cloth wound at the highest leg-joint. The bird's wings can do little for balance. The next day the bird does not come even though the baby waits and waits until the sun sinks below the bassinet's rim and a cool evening breeze slips its hand over his cheek. For days after he searches the empty sky, finding nothing but the scudding movement of clouds, a soft rain that soaks the meadow. Later the baby will remember the bird like a dream: brown-feathered, light as a love note. He will recall its forked tail, its wings through which the light shone. The body limned with light.

Each Moment Sufficient Unto Itself

He looks troubled
when he sleeps, and I find
I cannot trust him. Can't trust

the breaths that
inflate/deflate the lungs, the lungs
that required *a small push*
to start up.

These mindless repetitions,
how each day resembles its others.

As if, by force of will, I could recall them.

I confess that I cannot see
a way forward. Submit your requests

to the proper authorities, affix
your virtual signature
to each virtual form.

I'd kept wishing to go to sleep,
and then the baby could be born, which is
essentially what took place.

Everything you say
will be used against you.

The afternoon we come home
from the hospital is hot and gray.
Rain threatens

but does not fall.
Light pools on an open page.

The phone rings and a voice says
be calm. You are not going to die.
These things happen.

Meanwhile, the toast is getting cold.

Notes and Acknowledgments

The publications in which these poems first appeared, some in slightly different forms or with different titles, are gratefully acknowledged:

Jellyfish: "Poem in Which a Decision Has Been Reached"; *Memorious:* "Postpartum"; *Mom Egg Review:* "Anterograde," "Postlude," "What It Is Like"; *Rogue Agent:* "Each Moment Sufficient Unto Itself"; *Salamander:* "Blood Orange"; *Thimble:* "Ghost of a Ghost."

"Poem in Which a Decision Has Been Reached" was also published in the chapbook *Not If But When* (Salt Hill, 2016).

Like the first epigraph, the phrase *"maternity, [the body] suffering for another"* in "Mornings Like This One" is from Emmanuel Levinas's *Otherwise Than Being.*

J.L. Conrad is the author of the full-length poetry collections *A World in Which* (Terrapin Books) and *A Cartography of Birds* (Louisiana State University Press), as well as the chapbooks *Recovery* (Texas Review Press, winner of the 2022 Robert Phillips Chapbook Prize) and *Not If But When* (Salt Hill, winner of the third annual Dead Lake Chapbook Competition). Her poems have appeared in *Pleiades, Sugar House Review, Salamander, Jellyfish, Beloit Poetry Journal*, and elsewhere. She lives in Madison, Wisconsin.

About Small Harbor Publishing

Small Harbor Publishing is a 501c3 nonprofit organization. Our goal is to publish unique and diverse voices. We are a feminist press, and we are committed to diversity and inclusion. We strive to bring new voices to a devoted and expanding readership.

Small Harbor Publishing began in 2018 with the first issue of *Harbor Review*. The magazine is an online space where poetry and art converse. *Harbor Review* quickly grew and now publishes reviews and runs multiple micro chapbook competitions, including the Washburn Prize and the Editor's Prize.

In July 2020, Small Harbor Publishing was officially incorporated and began Harbor Editions. Harbor Editions accepts submissions through a chapbook open reading period, a hybrid chapbook open reading period, the Marginalia Series, and the Laureate Prize.

In 2023, Harbor Anthologies began with a mission to promote texts that explore social justice issues and highlight marginalized writers.

If you would like to support Small Harbor Publishing, visit our "About" page at: smallharborpublishing.com/about.